Beautiful Imperfection

Beautiful Imperfection

Finding Light in Unexpected Places

Jennifer Robyn

I respectfully acknowledge those who walk beside me and those who have gone before me, including the traditional owners of the land where I live and work.

I am grateful to Wendy Bailye for generously sharing her photographs from Minjerribah (Stradbroke Island). A sincere thankyou to Susie Blue for the design.

The reflections in this work are based on the author's life experiences and observations. Names have been changed to protect the privacy of friends and relatives.

ISBN 978-1-7638431-1-0

Author contact details: jenniferrobyn187@gmail.com

Digital art created using photos by Wendy Bailye and images from the author's family collection.
Design by Susie Blue.

Printed by Ingram Spark.

Thankyou to my dear friends and family

who lovingly share my journey.

Preface

The search for light, for being surprised by the beauty of our humanity within the darkness and the ordinariness of life, has snuck up on me. I wasn't expecting to begin to notice glimpses of human kindness and joy, of love and learning — things that have always been there, but I haven't had the eyes to see them.

From the early years, to the twilight years, and everything in between, I have come to accept that when life takes me by the shoulders and shakes me, it also shapes me. It has taken me most of my life to fit comfortably in this reflective space. Unexpected pleasure, moments of love and light in the darkness, insights that rattle my cage — all of it weaves itself into the tapestry that becomes my life's **_Beautiful Imperfection_**.

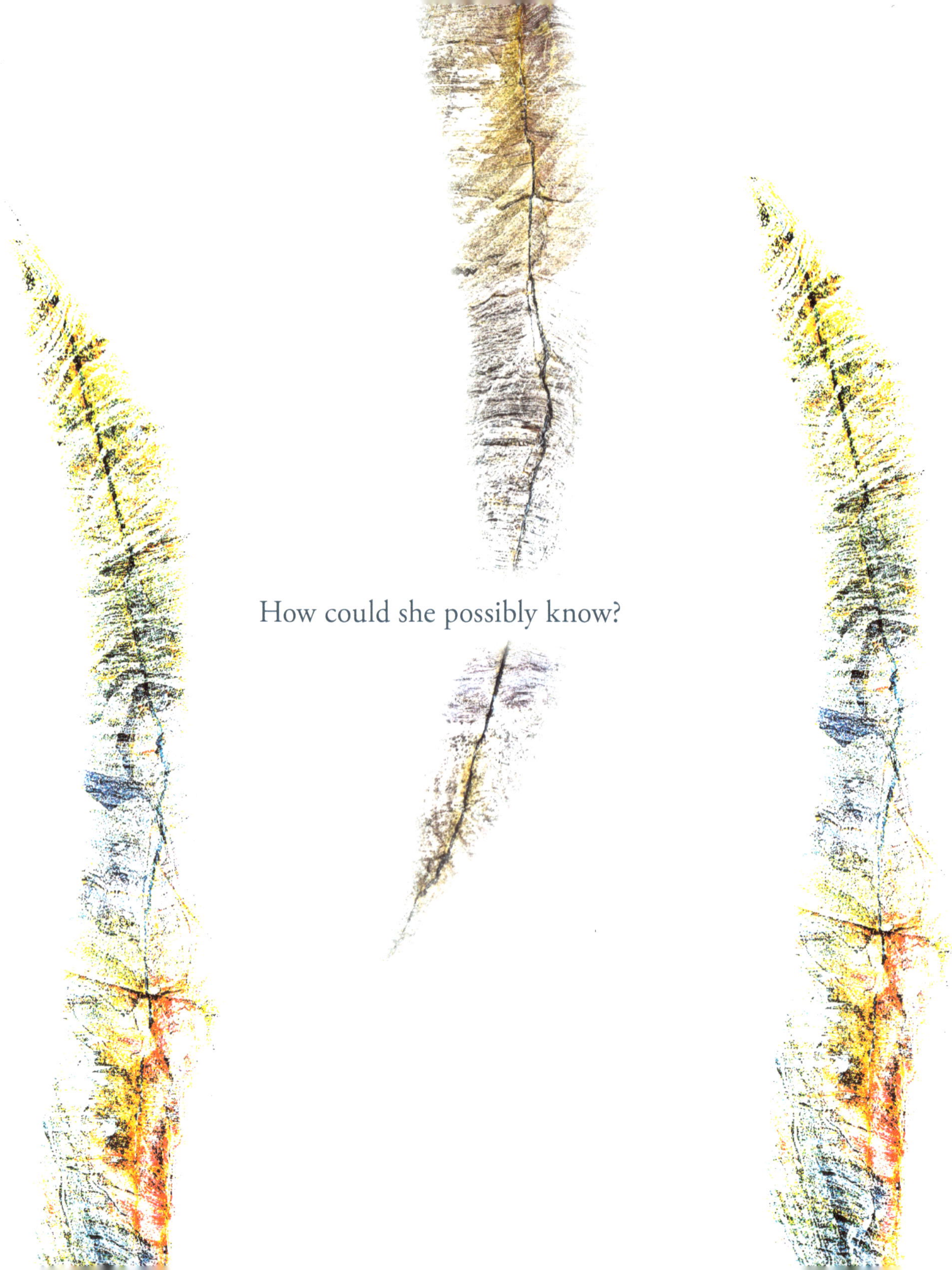

How could she possibly know?

Not in her Job Description

I'm aware of the stranger who is me, stunned, wandering, staring but not seeing, unable to choose what to put in the trolley, oblivious of the other shoppers or the PA announcements urging someone to the front desk. Barely remembering to breathe.

Karen is repacking shelves when our eyes connect. She's worked there a long time, always giving a friendly hello to everyone she serves. She enjoys connecting with the customers, most of whom she knows by name.

As grocery shopping is part of my weekly routine, in my time of turmoil I grasp for the mundane. I am a regular, but this day Karen frowns.

'Are you ok love?'

How could she possibly know?

In the deserted aisle, her gentle eyes understand as I blurt out the recent horror that should belong to someone else on the TV news.

The chilled air, the obscure music, the customer traffic all blur in time. It only takes a minute, maybe two. I move on, dazed and shaky, but cradling her soothing words.

'Now you take care, love.'

The shelves resume their everyday order. Who would have thought that those simple words would create a safe place for a troubled soul to gather a few groceries?

Stack. Greet. Swipe. Run-of-the-mill chit chat. That's her routine. We still see each other at the checkout every week, but there's no need to talk about that day. Her smile and the nod say everything.

The Wedding

Our daughter Cara asked us to take the girls for a few days. I hear the urgency in her voice.

'Of course! Of course!' Lord only knows our girl needs some time for herself.

So, it's arranged. Our wedding anniversary fell on the Friday. What was it — 43 or 44 years? I lose track. We usually go out to a swanky Japanese restaurant and toast our good fortune.

Never mind. There's always next year.

⌣

I'm at home with the two girls as Pop heads off to work. They're generally with us on the weekends, when he takes them spotlighting, creating the bonfire and teaching them to drive the ride-on. The grandchildren and I have our own favourite things to do — cooking, craft, reading or exploring the flavours of the vegie patch.

What will we do today? I usually follow their lead. When I tell the girls about our anniversary, their eyes light up.

'We could have a wedding!'

First, we plan the menu. Fried Rice and trifle. They throw themselves into the prep-work while balancing on the stools at the kitchen bench. Next, costumes. It's amazing what can be created with scarves, mosquito net and old lace curtains. My two little bridesmaids swirl in front of the mirror and endlessly rearrange their outfits. On my wedding day, I carried frangipani, white ones with pale yellow centres. Out in the yard, we break off a few from the row of fragrant trees and wrap the stems in foil to stop the white milk.

The day is getting away from us and there's still more to do. Shuffling through the CDs, I stumble across Michael Bublé singing the Stevie Wonder song, *You and I*. It's perfect.

I ask the girls what they think we should promise. At this stage I wasn't really sure we should be going down the rabbit hole of wedding vows, but the game had taken on a life of its own and they scribbled in their note books.

～

The wrinkled bride under the mosquito net shuffles her way along the hallway toward her silver-haired groom. Two brightly decked-out bridesmaids lead the way clutching their frangipani posies, looking more like belly dancers than bridesmaids, while Bublé croons about how, together, we can conquer the world with love.

Solemnly the little ones look up at us and say, 'Repeat after me.'

'I will always help you.' *I will always help you.*

'I will always look after you.' *I will always look after you.*

'I will never leave you.' *I will never leave you.*

'I will always love you.' *I will always love you.*

We choke out the words through our tears. And as the four of us swayed to the fading tones of our wedding song, I knew that this was the best wedding anniversary ever.

Red Flags

Keeping our heads low, we hoped that nobody had noticed us, but our tears were in plain sight. Two silver-haired oldies in the front row with hands folded like obedient children.

It was the end of a huge day of exhibits and activities, designed to entice new families to the school. A pedal-powered slushy machine, quad bike riding and cattle branding drew our grandkids and Cara, away from the formal presentation about the school's ethos and values, but we needed to know what this school stood for.

Cara had asked us to come to the open day as her eyes and ears, her sounding board, her secret sensors. Was there a high school to understand, to educate while supporting our family? That's what we were there to find out.

Such unexpected truth had us rattled …

As we braced for the principal's spiel to parents, we anticipated the *Blah, Blah, Blah* of self-promotion.

Thirty-five years ago, we were seduced by the glossy brochures which promised that our children would reach their full potential. What a disappointment. Our red flags were carefully concealed, twitching to be brandished at the first whiff of hypocrisy.

The principal was not a physically imposing man, dressed conservatively in dark trousers and a long-sleeved pastel shirt and tie. Seated and relaxed, with the air of confidence and authority which accompany his position, he began.

'I don't know about you, but I find that schools generally let kids down.'

We dared a furtive glance, steeling ourselves for the catch. We know the routine — say something to hook the audience, then reel them in.

Pleased with the attention he had commanded, he continued.

'We've all witnessed little kids skipping into the early years of learning, open and keen to discover the world.'

We nodded our agreement.

'But then our education system manages to stifle their thirst for learning. By the time they come to us at high school, most kids are disengaged, turned off school and would probably say that being with their friends was the highlight of their day.'

Such unexpected truth had us rattled. The principal and the head of teaching and learning went on to describe how their *Every Kid Counts* philosophy finds expression in daily classroom practices.

We kept listening for the catch — the behaviour management three-point plan, the expectation of adopting the school's faith-based underpinnings, the veiled threats to parents to keep their kids in line or else! But our flags remained furled and out of sight as the presentation continued.

'No child at this school will be humiliated by being asked a question when it's clear that the answer is beyond them. You know, I interview many teachers who want to work here, many with impressive qualifications and experience, but if they haven't got a heart for kids, I don't want them anywhere near my school!'

That's when the tears spilled over. They were unexpected and unstoppable.

We cried for our own missed opportunities at school.

We cried for our kids, and how schooling had let them down, but mostly our tears flowed in a flood of relief and gratitude at the possibility of a safe, nurturing place for our grandchildren to learn and flourish.

The Companion

Ned never imagined himself as a father. The responsibility was inconceivable. His complex, colourful life bounced around from day to day, with no regard to roots or permanency. Perhaps the time was never quite right. Even well into his thirties he lived on the edge, dodging the law and scraping together enough cash to survive.

While life was random, there had never been a choice about fishing. He'd had a line in his hand since he was a toddler in his grandfather's boat. Those undisturbed days on the bay shaped a safe, quiet, inner place in which to retreat when life was challenging and unpredictable.

In a sometimes-chaotic world, fishing was always a constant. Having a best-mate fishing partner was a bonus. A girl who likes baiting a hook and dragging in a catch is a rare find, and their lives had an easy unregulated flow until the day he sheepishly announced their news to us. Fear and uncertainty overshadowed his face. We glowed at the thought of another grandchild.

By the river bank, his little one was used to playing alone under the sprawling Moreton Bay Fig while they fished nearby. With no siblings, Leah had become an expert in creating the most wonderful imaginary world among the crusty roots and rough bark. It was a magical place full of fairies and little people with houses and furniture created out of twigs and dried leaves.

Cradling a treasure in her tiny warm palm, she sauntered up to her dad saying cheekily,

'Hey Dad! Would you like some company?'

Somewhat taken aback, Ned nodded with secret pleasure. Passing on the fishing tradition would be a joy.

'There you are,' she announced.
'Here's a pet rock.'

Leah lovingly laid her warmed, companion gift beside his tackle box.

As he observed his daughter scampering back to her tree, wispy, spider-web hair flying in the breeze, Ned smiled to himself, marvelling at how such a precious little being had captured his heart from the moment she had come into his world.

Silent Night

Something happens to the eyes of children in the lead up to Christmas. They widen with wonder and anticipation to the point where they engulf their eager young faces and then become almost wild with excitement as the calendar crawls towards the big day.

Our rural neighbourhood has a tradition of gathering together, a few days before the whirlwind of celebrations takes over. It's just a few of us in our quiet street who enjoy this casual catch up enough to keep the tradition going. We lug our camping chairs and eskies with food and drink to share, sometimes relaxing in a cooling evening breeze and sometimes scurrying under cover to escape a summer storm.

For a few years, we have all brought something to entertain the gathering — an improvised song about the neighbourhood, a bush poem, a martial arts demonstration, and even a guinea pig race with prizes for who could guess the winner. This year the kids are more focussed on toasting marshmallows and hurtling around the yard in the trailer of the ride-on mower so the instruments stay in their cases.

The night wears on. Most people drift off home having exhausted their news or reluctantly accepting that their little ones have run out of puff. A few remain around the dying embers so I unzip the guitar cover and start strumming and

humming *Silent Night*. It really is a silent night — still and cool with a heaven full of stars above us.

My neighbours are an interesting bunch, their lilting accents betraying their birth in faraway places, but it seems that *Silent Night* is sung all over the world. So here we are, under a canopy of stillness, singing in four languages.

> *Silent Night, Holy Night, All is calm, All is bright.*
>
> *Stille Nacht, heilige Nacht, Alles schläft; einsam wacht*
>
> *Stille nacht, heilige nacht, Alles slaapt, sluimert zacht.*
>
> *Stilla natt, heliga natt! Allt är frid. Stjärnan blid*

That's when I notice her eyes.

Willa has remained with the adults, curled up on her mother's lap, observing intently. She's only about nine years old, but wise enough to recognise that the familiar carol is being sung in multiple languages simultaneously. There are no gifts or sparkling trees or tinsel decorations to capture her awe, just a few neighbours singing together, yet when the magic of this moment engulfs us all, her brown eyes sparkle like the stars above on that calm, bright night.

Books and Covers

The Good Stuff ideas forum settled into its second meeting. The theme for the month was friendship. We shared stories, poems and songs about good friends, old friends, forgotten friends, superficial friends. Questions were posed about what constitutes a lasting friendship and why some people come and go in our lives. Can friendships survive a change in basic beliefs or a world view? Should we trot after people who disappear off our radar, fearful of having to cross anyone off our diminishing friends list? Maybe the question to be most afraid of is: Am I a friend worth having?

The flow of ideas was relaxed and earnest, with all but one contributing. Earlier, at the beginning of the session, it was impossible not to notice the young woman, Tanya, shuffling through the door with her carer, resting her walking stick in the corner. As group leader, I was slightly anxious that she may not feel included. Tanya wasn't passive, but deeply engaged, her sharp eyes flitting from speaker to speaker, drinking it all in.

In a lull, she spoke. Slowly. Very slowly and deliberately. All heads turned. Her disability was laid bare, but her carefully chosen words hung over the table.

'I think it's important to know and accept yourself.'

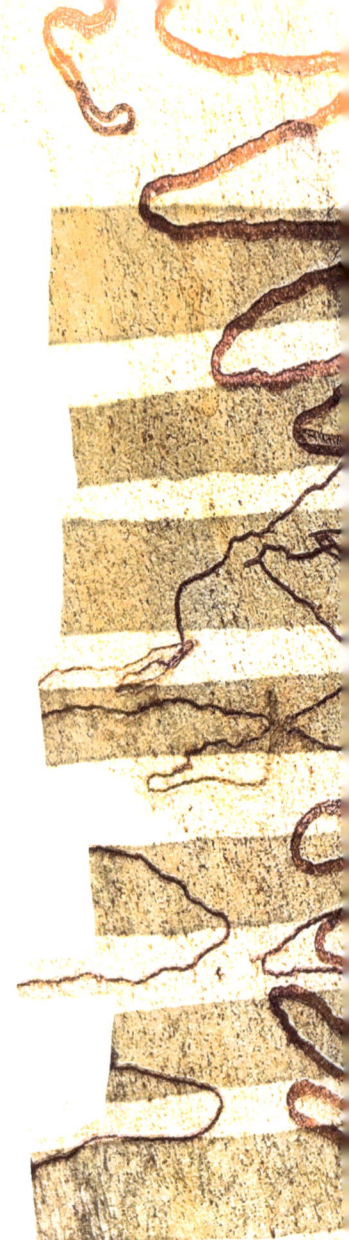

She obviously had more to say, so we waited for the words to form.

'If you know yourself, then it doesn't matter if people come into your life and leave your life.'

With great effort, she concluded.

'So just be true to yourself. That's what counts.'

Stunned silence. Her words cut through as though nothing else mattered. Such wisdom so carefully delivered. For me on that day, I saw Tanya for the first time. An intelligent, humble and thoughtful young woman. A wise one to be listened to and respected.

I marvel with gratitude that life goes on surprising me, and sometimes jolting me when I least expect it.

her words cut through … nothing else mattered …
… intelligent, humble and thoughtful …

Imperfect Pleasure

I've owned a guitar since my teens. My playing is plonkity-plonk — strumming chords so I can sing along to the tunes of Bob Dylan or Don McLean. A friend, an accomplished guitarist, hearing the tone of my old gal, tells me I have a very nice instrument indeed. I'm surprised. That's when I decide to honour her by taking lessons. Fifty years too late.

My initial lesson is a litany of what I can't do.

'I can't read music. I don't know the name of the strings. I don't know the notes on the fret board. I can only play chords from memory.'

Joel comes highly praised so I'm ready to trust him. He smiles sympathetically.

'Doesn't matter. Don't worry about that.
Let's just start with this.'

I feel like a five year old learning to read. Week by week the squiggles on the page begin to make sense. Joel's quiet commentary is always positive even though I don't measure up to my own perfect standards.

'You're mastering this passage beautifully. You really have the sense of the tango rhythm.'

When I rush because of nerves, Joel quietly plays along, with slender fingers perching on the strings of his well loved guitar, slowing the rhythm, modelling the breathing.

I'm holding my breath again.

I'm thankful for this young man's patience and gentle coaching.

My old Italian guitar's shapely body sings and hums, swoons and demands attention in the tango. I can hear it in my head, but I stumble, fumble, make mistakes, go over and over it. Perfection eludes me. I have accepted that I will never perform in public, but the pleasure is in the hope of one day playing all or part of a piece beautifully.

When it works, I breathe out, exhaling the joy and satisaction. I don't want to play it again because I know that next time I'll stuff it up and put the guitar away in frustration.

I stumble, fumble, and make mistakes …

I shrink inside with the insecurity of such an announcement …

My new challenge is by Phil Houghton, an Australian guitarist and self-taught composer who took an unconventional route to classical music. The story goes that at nine he used his first guitar as a cricket bat, but later repaired his damaged instrument with glue and fishing line so he could imitate the legendary Jimmy Hendrix. Phil died too young, in his early sixties, but left behind an incredible legacy of compositions with influences ranging from Rock to Jazz to Classical. Maybe that diversity and unusual background is what attracts me to his music.

His *Black Rose Prelude* is melodic without an easily recognisable tune. It's soft yet dramatic. It draws me in. I get lost in the sounds, the shape — my fingers going where they should on the strings, except for that one stretch which sometimes sounds okay, but mostly jars the senses.

I feel nervous when I announce to Joel that I'm ready to show what I can do, but shrink inside with the insecurity of such an announcement, mindful of the liklihood I won't do it justice.

Will my fingers stretch?
Will I get so lost in the music that I lose my place?
Will my earnestness appear foolish?

The day comes to play *Black Rose Prelude*. I want to get it right. I want to show what I can do when I practise at home without an audience. As I gently tilt forward, draping my weight around my guitar, I become lost in beauty until the final notes roll off my thumb. I breath out a combination of relief and exhilaration. I feel I have honoured Phil's music.

Looking up, I'm sure Joel's dark eyes are misty. Perhaps he's saddened by the premature passing of the composer, or knows more of his story than I do. But I'm going to hang on to the illusion that maybe, just maybe, my playing moved him like it moved me.

Reframed

Nudity was frowned upon in my childhood home. Necklines were above the collar bone and dresses below the knee, except, in the sixties, when my miniskirts were reluctantly tolerated. This morality was highlighted when, as a young mum, I picnicked with extended family at the beach. The in-between weather meant that I had not packed swimmers for my littlies. As the temperature rose, so did their agitation to splash and paddle. As I stripped them off, I heard an admonishment from one of the rellies.

'Rudie Nudie. You'd better watch out! The policeman might come and get you.'

At the time, I ignored the comment, and the kids enjoyed the water, oblivious of judgement. But the incident triggered memories of my upbringing where modesty and an avoidance of discussion around anything sexual prevailed. Messages of purity, waiting for marriage and innocence shaped my cultural heritage.

～

Once known as *Wild Thing*, I was now lost in the fog of saucepans, mops and nappies, so the opportunity of a trip to Melbourne, on my own, was thrilling.

To kill time before my brother collected me from the city, I ventured into the National Gallery of Victoria which was hosting a Brett Whiteley retrospective. I knew about his *Sydney Harbour* paintings, but much of what I saw that day was unusual, if not confronting. Flicking through the souvenir posters in the gift shop I came across a print of Whiteley's wife, Wendy, entitled *Blue Nude*. I couldn't

… much of what I saw that day was unusual …

resist the wild, easy, free movement of her generous body so I shyly purchased my illicit poster which was, thankfully, rolled up in a cardboard tube for convenient transport home on the plane.

∽

Now, what to do?

Tucked away in the back of my wardrobe, was an ancient, empty timber frame, salvaged from my parent's house when they moved. It had belonged to my great-grandmother, Sarah Kate, but I have no idea of its original contents. With fine sandpaper and linseed oil, I removed generations of dust, revealing multiple layers of light and dark in the beautiful old timbers, and, as an act of defiance, I encased *Blue Nude* in Sarah Kate's frame, hanging it above my bed.

Then a bizarre thought surfaced.

What if my insolence liberates Sarah Kate? What if she is released from the Victorian constricts of her generation? I castigated myself for such a wacko idea, that the actions of the living could alter the consciousness of the dead, but secretly I dared to hope that I had set her free.

∽

Sometimes I observe my grandchildren creeping into my bedroom, giggling at grandma's picture. I'm glad they have noticed her.

Knowing and Not Knowing

Richard's retirement function was an informal catch-up of past and current work mates — a long-anticipated lunchtime reunion in the professional development space overlooking the river. His suit, ties and pressed business shirts were abandoned at the back of the wardrobe. Today he was dressed in snug jeans and his favourite cotton RM Williams country shirt, his silver-grey halo towering over the crowd. With so many colleagues attending, it was clear he was well liked and respected. Being someone who likes to be in control, I wondered how, on such a momentous occasion, he would handle his emotions.

As we walked arm in arm into the room, I searched for a familiar face. I hung back, shy yet eager to hear what was said about him when the formalities began. While my man appeared nonchalant, looking sheepish, hoping they were going to talk about someone else, I noticed the small beads of moisture on his brow, betraying his nerves.

'His door is always open. He's a good friend, a caring man.'

Well yes, that's my experience too. Before our romance blossomed, Richard was my best mate. Still to this day, I share my life with a faithful, loyal friend. And it's true, too, he is a caring person, but I also see the harshness. Standing his ground.

'You can hear his laugh along the corridor.'

Really? I haven't noticed his laugh. Does he laugh at home? Are we too serious? We should have more fun.

'He's a deeply intelligent person who can explain complex concepts patiently, in terms that others can understand. He never big-notes himself but shares his knowledge with generosity and humility.'

It was clear, even in the early days, Richard's wisdom ran deep. The day after our joyful wedding, accompanied by so many guitars and songs it resembled a concert, the enormity of it all hit me.

'What have we done! What if we've made a mistake?' Without pausing, he said,

'Well, we'll just have to make sure every day that we haven't.'

Such wisdom from one so young. I was reassured. I felt safe.

∾

The accolades from colleagues past and present continued, at times tearfully.

'He's a patient man. Kind and thoughtful.'

When I told the kids that they said he was a patient man, our son quipped,

'I taught him that!' It's true.

In a culture where we aren't usually comfortable with back-slapping, layer upon layer of praise was served up, but the end of a career is the ideal occasion to say good things about the person leaving and I didn't begrudge any of it. I beamed — my pride for him on show.

There was a slight wobble in his confidence when Richard stepped up to respond. His carefully crafted speech followed a chronological order, starting with an acknowledgement of support from his 'home team'. That's me. I was unprepared for the emotion. Looking away, taking his time, he steadied and continued, thanking and acknowledging his colleagues, past and present.

By the end of the speeches, it was as though I'd been peeking through a window into a stranger's life. I thought: This man is a saint! We've shared love and passion, children, companionship and friendship, hurt and healing, but even after all this time, is it possible to really know another?

I've heard marriage described as a journey, a partnership, but for me this long union is like being on different journeys yet on the same path. Alone yet not alone.

The speeches and the alcohol left a haze of goodwill in the room. As an outsider, I observed my man from a distance. Was he really the same person who stood beside me in his purple trousers and matching patterned shirt? No suit coat for my groom. In my simple white cotton-voile dress, with corn-coloured tresses adorned with frangipani, we looked like we'd only recently been children.

In our youth and innocence, we sounded confident and sure of ourselves.

I give you this ring

Wear it with love and joy

I choose you to be my husband

This day and every day.

We had no idea what these words would mean. When we were young and wise, we used to say that the only thing in life you can be sure about is change. I think we were right.

Kookaburra Sisters

At Mum's funeral, I delivered the eulogy. Love of family and deep faith were at her core, but just as memorable was her raucous laugh. It was inescapable. In my words, I said that whenever I heard the kookaburras laughing, I thought of Bette and her three sisters, all of whom were blessed with that infectious cackle.

Memories resurfaced as the slides rolled through. Mum and my aunts Molly, Elsie, and Kitty sharing lunch every Tuesday at Ma's house. As pre-schoolers, we kids played under the tank stand, where all we could hear was ripple upon ripple of laughter. But what was there to laugh about? The sisterhood shared burdens of an unhappy marriage, early widowhood and the exhaustion of being a mum of four children under five. Elsie probably felt grateful for her single status. I wonder if laughter was their salvation.

All talk would cease at 1pm. Dishes had to be cleared and a reverent hush descended over the dining table because that's when the whole nation came to a standstill for the long-running radio series *Blue Hills*. I remember giggling with my cousins at the dramatic voices of those iconic characters. Even today, that theme music draws up nostalgia in me.

⌒

A new slide in the funeral photo tribute, and now I'm the grandma. As we tried to capture the four generations, our daughter's little one kept poking her finger up her nose. The more we laughed and admonished her, the further up the nose the digit explored. Mum's laughter became a cascade as we roared convulsively, eyes streaming, shoulders shuddering. That's the moment the camera clicked. It's my favourite photo of Mum.

It was after her death, and around the time of our own family trauma, that the strange kookaburra visitations began.

I wonder if laughter was their salvation?

The bird shows up, perching on the balustrade, too close for a wild bird. We know the rules — don't feed the wild life, but it comes back again and again. I start to feel annoyed and even find myself talking to the stupid bird.

'It's alright Mum. We're ok. You don't have to keep checking up on us. We'll get through this.'

I worked hard to establish an adult relationship with my mum. Maintaining my independence, at the same time resisting my mum's sometimes overwhelming need to mother, was a challenge.

At first, I reject the impossible thought that the tug-of-war is continuing in the form of a wild bird. But there it is again. At every family barbecue, balancing on the back of a chair, refusing to be shushed away. Becoming a real pest!

At last, the bird and I have serious words.

'I know you care about us Mum, but we are strong. We'll get through this together.' And then a new idea. Maybe she wants to let me know she's ok too. My tone softens as I address the bird once more.

'Do you understand now, Mum? I needed distance to become me? Do you get it now, Mum? Every parent has to learn how to be with their adult children. I'm learning it with my kids now. It's not easy.'

The wise, knowing eyes stare me down. I considered my ruminations with the kookaburra resolved, put away in the bottom draw with the old photos, but then my restlessness throws up something new. In some cultures, a visitation in the form of a fluffy bird with penetrating, intelligent eyes would be expected.

So why is it such a conundrum for me?

So much to ponder. So much to learn.

In the Moment

Elsie, my favourite aunt, was tall and shapely, carrying herself with a dignity belying her working-class beginnings. She was a real looker! She sewed all her own clothes and always looked smart, wearing just the right outfit for the occasion, including hats and gloves. It's surprising what a small girl notices. But I was drawn to her because of her self-sufficiency, as well as her poise, her grace, and her ability to appear calm and capable regardless of the circumstances.

Despite her charming attributes she was single, although she didn't fit the old maid stereotype. There was some talk of a 'disappointment' during the war, but the details were never revealed to us children, and by the time I was an adult, it wasn't my place to ask. The truth was, Aunty didn't need anyone to make her life complete.

How cruel and unfair that such a sophisticated, capable woman should end her days in a narrow room of a deteriorating nursing home. To compensate for feeling like I was abandoning her, I scattered the room with familiar things — faded photos in gilded frames, her crystal dressing table set placed on ironed, self-embroidered doylies. But nothing could camouflage the starkness of peeling paint in these decaying surroundings of Sunset Gardens. One lone tree was framed by her window. At each visit, we repeated the same banter.

'Come over here to the window.

Have you ever seen such a beautiful tree? It's big isn't it!'

'Yes, Aunty. It's a lovely tree.' I keep the impatience out of my voice.

'How are you going anyway? Is everything alright?'

'Oh, yes. They're lovely. They take good care of me here. I can't complain.'

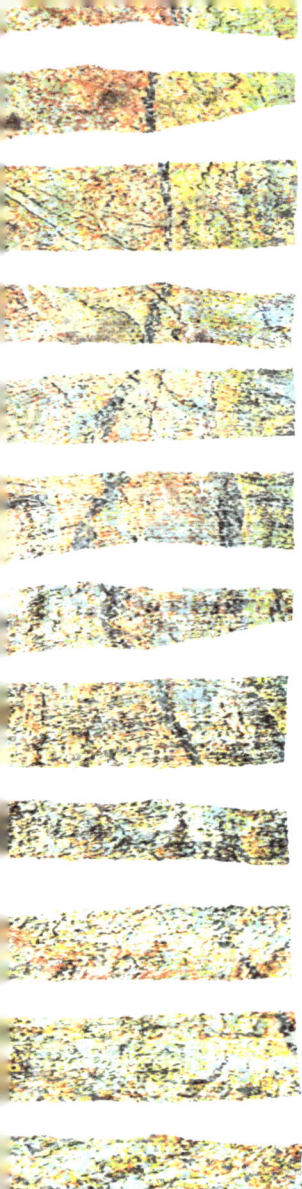

… lulling the chrysalises with far away eyes,
… waiting patiently for their transformation.

Then her sly sense of humour kicked in with a chuckle.

'Who'd listen, anyway?'

My repulsion of that place collided with her gracious acceptance and appreciation of the care she received there.

Toward the end of her time, I attended the Christmas party. It was a jolly affair, with a troupe of overly-bright, happy musicians entertaining those who were present enough to engage, while lulling the chrysalises with far away eyes, lying dormant, waiting patiently for their transformation. Some staff danced with a few of the rickety residents.

Elsie entwined her frail fingers with mine and, with elbows resting on the table, we rocked our locked hands side to side to the beat, while her watery sapphire eyes searched for faded memories that refused to surface.

For the last song of the concert, the up-beat mood relaxed as the performers moved into an old-time country favourite by Kris Kristofferson. As I scanned the room, I was drawn into the lyrics of *One Day at a Time.*

That's all I'm asking … help me to take … one day at a time.

In front of me was humanity in all its forms: singing, swaying, looking happy. I gazed into my aunt's pale blue distant eyes and saw once more that quiet, self-contained, independent woman that I loved.

This was the last time I saw her. She passed away soon after. But there remains a shimmering memory of that day which continues to call me to be more like her.

Mr. Fix It

Mr. Fix It was the man you went to if you wanted something done. He sought out people who needed help and was happiest when he had a project. Even in our adult years, we, his children, could recite back to him his favourite sayings.

'If a job's worth doing, it's worth doing well.

Don't put off to tomorrow, what you can do today.

Do it NOW!'

As he aged, Dad still tackled projects but, of necessity, they had to be less physically and mentally taxing, like dabbling in his little garden, or churning up compost with aged manure from the local pony club. The bank, Centrelink, and other government bodies probably didn't have too many 95-year-olds emailing them or calling to clarify the many hurdles that pensioners have to navigate.

Mr. Fix It's identity was inseparable from his ability to make things happen, so even when he received the cancer diagnosis, he really didn't believe it would change anything. He still walked two kilometres a day, did his own shopping and delighted in experimenting in the kitchen. After Mum passed away, like a mischievous kid, he broke her kitchen conventions, always mindful of her distant expert eye observing his unusual creations. Bette would never have tipped a can of baked beans in with a few scrambled eggs, but, according to Dad, it was a success. People always remarked, *you're marvellous for your age* and you could tell he soaked up the compliment.

The insidious enemy within his bones wouldn't be deigned, as gradually Mr Fix It ran out of puff. With a sense of resignation, he packed his bag. Feeling miserable, yet using my most businesslike voice I suggested,

'What about warm socks, Dad? Sometimes the aircon in hospitals is quite cool.'

He carefully folded track pants, t-shirts and a pull-over into his overnight bag. His worn bible snuggled down between his pyjamas and undies. The radio and toiletries found their place neatly into the side pocket. Dad's upbeat tone was betrayed by his drooping shoulders and downcast eyes.

'Come on love. Let's do this.'

I couldn't meet his eyes. I felt like Judas.

On the drive to St Vincent's Hospital, he sang to himself the old Spiritual: *Swing Low. Sweet Chariot. Comin' for to carry me home.* I was driving so didn't dare let my tears tumble as I struggled to join in. It was clear he had accepted the inevitable — that an admission to a Palliative Care Unit was most likely his final stop.

Over a week or so, the palliative specialists hit on the right cocktail of drugs to mask his pain and Dad started sitting up in the chair, chatting about life and the test cricket to the cleaner, the nurse, the physio, the social worker, the specialist doctors — anyone who would listen. They used to say that coming to his room was the highlight of their day. When he was discharged with his bundle of prescriptions, the cleaner shed a tear, while the other staff waved him on his way with their blessing and reassurance of ongoing palliative support.

'Don't forget, Dan. We're only a phone call away.'

Dad knows that he doesn't have much time left, but even though he can't physically fix much these days, he has brought life to those who care for the dying. That's what's left when you can't fix anything anymore.

Raw Love

Around his grave, arms drooped across each other's shoulders, the four of us faced the undeniable truth that we were now officially orphans. In the shade of the slanting paper bark, grandchildren and great-grandchildren joined us, silent, with bowed heads. So close to death, the intimacy was tangible.

Dad was gone and we would all miss him terribly yet the overwhelming sense was: This is a good ending to a full, loving life. There was nothing left unsaid. Nothing left undone. What more could anyone want?

For seven years, deep in the earth, Mum had waited patiently for the love of her life to join her. We were grateful our parents had lived such long and fruitful lives, still devoted to each other till death us do part.

As we grew into adulthood, they used to muse,

'How did we produce four kids who are so different?'

It's true, when you look at some families, they seem like clones. But not us. On that solemn day, we each offered our unique gifts to honour Dad.

For me, it was words and reflections. Thomas, our priest/brother, brought liturgy and structure. Bonny offered family memories and a connection to the spirituality that she shared with Mum and Dad.

Then there was Andrew. The youngest. How could we include him in a meaningful way with our ceremonies and rituals? With his builder's back constantly reminding him of his life of hard physical work, Andrew endures constant pain. The inability to read, too, has always hung over him, like a curse to be ashamed of, more so now that he is almost blind. These days his life has shrunk to a room in his daughter's house, the wild and wonderful freedom of riding the waves is just a cherished memory.

Determined not to sideline him in the shadow of his siblings, I phoned ahead of the funeral.

'Hey, Andy. How are you doing?'

'Yeah. Ok. Thanks, Jen. You know… It was inevitable that the old fella would go eventually.'

'Yes. Ninety-eight isn't a bad innings. And he wasn't in pain.' I paused, waiting to see if he had anything else to say.

'I just wanted to fill you in on the details for the burial followed by the memorial service at the church. Is there anything you'd like to say or do?'

His response was immediate.

'No. Don't ask me to say anything. But I'll be there. You can count on me to be there.'

'I thought you might like to carry Dad's ashes and place them in the hole at the cemetery.'

'I'd probably drop them,' he said with a chuckle.

'Well, Tom and Bonnie and I can speak on your behalf at the church service, but burying ashes, well this is bloke's business, Andy.'

'Ok. I'll do it, if you think I can.'

… threads of love, loss and gratitude, woven into our living tapestry.

I'm glad I pushed back.

The ashes carry their own story. Dad had purchased the cemetery plot in Hemmant where he had buried Mum. He thought he would die in Brisbane too. But when my sister and her husband suggested they could look after him in Mackay, he accepted their offer and, after six months, passed away in their loving care.

I brought his ashes back on the plane — a 5kg bundle that, fortunately, didn't raise eyebrows with airport security. The urn was beautiful to look at and to touch. A smooth, ceramic replica of a grey pebble-like rock was the obvious choice for Dad, the rock of our family. One of Dad's grandchildren labelled the journey as *Poppa's Ashes Tour.* As a cricket fanatic, he would have worn that description with pride.

∾

The morning was chilly. A slight breeze fluttered the leaves of the paper bark as Tom, in his black cassock, recited the funeral prayers. As his resonant voice faded, we waited for Andrew, our eyes fixed on the square, shallow hole in the ground.

Edging close to the hole, Andy dropped to his knees. Tenderly, he raised the rock to his lips and kissed it, saying, 'I love you, Dad.' Then with great care, he placed the urn into the hole.

Andrew gripped his back as he struggled to his feet, still gazing at the ashes.

Silence. Reverence. Unspoken gratitude to our brother who brought raw love to our father's grave.

Not one, but two grandchildren are landscapers, so it fell to them to shovel the dirt and carefully stamp down the surface, like professional gardeners. When the hole was half full, I noticed the piece of paper in the small hand next to mine.

'Stop! Stop! Stop!'

When someone is filling in a grave, you don't yell out *Stop!*

What's the matter? Aren't they dead? Ashes are pretty final!

Twenty pairs of eyes brimming with tears looked up in alarm.

'The children. They have brought messages to place in the grave with Poppa.'

The placing of cards and messages was not part of the regular liturgy, and in the busyness of preparations, this gesture had been overlooked.

As we recovered from the pause in the ceremony, the little ones moved forward, dropping their memories into the hole. Raised eyebrows gave way to grateful, relieved nods and smiles, while the landscapers respectfully finished their work.

On that sombre morning, our parents would have been proud of us.

Young children side by side with parents, uncles, aunts and grandparents — without words, all of us sensing something bigger than anything we could see or touch. Death, threads of love, loss and gratitude, woven into our living tapestry.

It felt complete — finished. Satisfying. Resolved.

No need to look back. No regrets.